To my wonderful family – for their unstinting support and patience

Published in November 2014
by Thomson Reuters (Professional) UK Limited
European Lawyer Reference Series
Friars House, 160 Blackfriars Road, London SE1 8EZ
(Registered in England & Wales, Company No 1679046.
Registered Office and address for service:
2nd floor, Aldgate House, 33 Aldgate High Street, London EC3N 1DL)

A CIP catalogue record for this book is available from the British Library.

ISBN:9780414038882

Thomson Reuters and the Thomson Reuters logo are trade marks of
Thomson Reuters.
Macfarlanes and the Macfarlanes logo are trade marks of Macfarlanes LLP.

Crown copyright material is reproduced with the permission of the Controller of
HMSO and the Queen's Printer for Scotland.

© 2014 David Berman

CONTENTS

PREFACE   **7**
David Berman

GUEST FOREWORD   **9**
Richard Brearley

1. INTRODUCTION   **11**

Contextual overview and objective

2. REGULATORY FRAMEWORK OVERVIEW   **13**

A. Regulatory requirements   13

B. Broader regulatory expectations   15

C. Sanctions available to the Regulator   16

    Link to 'fitness and propriety'   17

D. Enforcement considerations   17

    'May'   18

    'Personal culpability'   19

    Case studies   21

        What do 'reasonable steps' look like?   21

        John Pottage v The Financial Services Authority,   22
        Upper Tribunal, 2012

        John Cummings – where the steps taken were   24
        not 'reasonable'

E. Directors' dilemma   25

    Legal context   25

    Regulatory backdrop   26

    Relative risk assessment   27

F. New 'Senior Persons' regime   27

3. CODE OF PRACTICE FOR APPROVED PERSONS 29

SP 5   30

  Apportionment and reporting lines   30

  Suitability of individuals   30

  Temporary vacancies   31

SP 6   36

  Knowledge of the business   36

  Delegation   36

SP 7   41

4. PRACTICALITIES – GOING BEYOND THE CODE OF PRACTICE 47

A. Practical considerations – general   47

  The importance of 'demonstrability'   47

  Adopting the right mind-set   48

  Handling regulatory interviews   49

    What to expect   49

    Preparation   50

    Key messages to be conveyed   50

    Dos and don'ts during the interview   51

  Setting the right 'tone from the top'   51

B. Practical considerations – specific SIF roles   52

  Chief Executive Officer (CF3)   52

    Initial assessments   52

    Other 'take-aways' from recent enforcement cases involving CEOs   53

    Culture   53

    Attestations   55

  Director (CF1)   55

Dichotomy of interests   56

Striking the right balance   56

Practicalities   58

Conclusion   59

Non-Executive Director (CF2)   60

Compliance Oversight (CF10)   62

5. ATTESTATIONS   63

Backdrop   63

Applicable regulation   64

Analysis   65

Mitigating the risk – practicalities   65

Conclusion   66

6. CONCLUDING REMARKS   67

Disclaimer

While it is hoped that this handbook serves as a helpful practical guide for SIF holders, it does not constitute legal advice. Every situation faced by a SIF holder in practice will be characterised by its own particular set of facts and circumstances – upon which the legal/regulatory analysis is ultimately likely to turn. Accordingly, professional advice should be sought in specific cases and scenarios.

PREFACE

The global banking crisis precipitated a deluge of reactive politically-motivated regulation – much of which is viewed as populist, ineffective and counter-intuitive. Nonetheless, authorised firms and regulated individuals[1] must 'play ball' if they are to continue to operate in the regulated financial services sector – however burdensome that may be in practice.

In the aftermath of the banking crisis, the Regulator was subjected to scathing criticism from politicians and media alike for failing to bring to book those presiding over the financial institutions that went to the brink and required bailouts. Perhaps unsurprisingly, therefore, a prominent feature of the UK Regulator's response has been a heightened and more concerted focus on senior individual accountability – a keen resolve to bring more Significant Influence Function (SIF) holders to account publicly for perceived regulatory contraventions and failings.

Against that backdrop, today's SIF holders are increasingly concerned about understanding the nature and extent of their regulatory responsibilities. A recurring theme among current (and prospective) SIFs is the desire for practical 'real world' guidance on how the applicable high-level regulatory principles (and associated evidential provisions) governing their roles translate into operational, day-to-day reality.

This handbook aims to bridge this 'rule to reality' gap, by providing practical guidance to SIF holders in identifying and managing their personal regulatory risk and potential liability. Indeed, it is hoped that SIF holders who take the approach, and adopt the mind-set, advocated will stand themselves in good stead *vis-à-vis* the Regulator; and accordingly minimise the prospects of attracting any adverse regulatory attention.

This handbook is of direct general relevance to **all** SIF roles. Certain (of the more common) SIF roles are also addressed separately – namely, the CF3 (CEO), CF1 (director), CF2 (non-executive director) and CF10 (compliance oversight) roles.

David Berman, October 2014

---

[1] Otherwise known as 'approved persons'.

GUEST FOREWORD

Richard Brearley

Senior individuals, including those who hold Significant Influence Functions (SIF), within financial service organisations are acutely aware that they have responsibilities and bear risks as a result of holding a senior position. The legal and regulatory frameworks, as well as society more generally, expects these important functions to be discharged effectively by senior individuals and we have seen a number of examples during and since the financial crisis, which serve to reinforce this view. However, to date, there has been a distinct lack of practical and authoritative guidance targeted specifically at SIF holders.

This handbook – written by a practitioner with significant industry and private practice experience – represents a welcome and timely development; and may well in time become 'standard issuance' for all SIF holders. Thought-provoking and insightful, the handbook takes a decidedly practical perspective, containing a host of valuable pointers and posing some deliberately provocative questions.

Helpfully, the handbook also directly addresses some of the key concerns preoccupying SIF holders in the current regulatory environment. Questions such as: What do I need to know? What is expected of me? How should I be conducting myself as a SIF holder? Where am I most exposed? What are the most likely avenues of challenge? How can I best protect myself?

For the first time, SIF holders have a practically-focused handbook at their disposal – a user-friendly reference guide through the morass of commonly-encountered issues and scenarios; and practical translation of prevailing regulatory expectations.

With regulatory risk and personal vulnerability high on the agenda for most, this handbook presents an intuitive and practicable framework, designed to help SIF holders mitigate such exposure down to acceptable levels.

Richard Brearley, Head of Legal and Compliance, Investec
September 2014

1

INTRODUCTION

Contextual overview and objective

At a time when expectations of boards and senior management have never been higher; and with a Regulator committed to bringing more senior level individuals to account, Significant Influence Function (SIF) holders are increasingly concerned about understanding the nature and extent of their regulatory responsibilities. However, this is not as simple as merely digesting the relevant high-level principles (and associated evidential provisions) contained within the rulebook – which will often bear little discernible resemblance to operational reality; and to those situations routinely encountered by SIF holders in practice[2].

This handbook aims to bridge this perceived 'rule to reality' gap; and answer – from a decidedly practical perspective – some of the key questions preoccupying SIF holders (and prospective SIF holders) in today's increasingly challenging regulatory environment:

- What do I need to know? What does the Regulator expect of me?
- What are the bounds of my responsibility?
- To what extent can I be held responsible for the (mis)conduct of others?
- How should I be conducting myself as a SIF holder? How far do I need to go?
- How should I approach regulatory interviews?
- Where am I most potentially vulnerable, in practice? What are the Regulator's most likely avenues of challenge? How can I best

---

[2] Indeed, in its evidence to the House of Commons Banking Standards Committee (in 2013), the FSA acknowledged that *"Assessing the reasonableness of steps which have been taken necessarily involves issues of judgment, and is not always straightforward. While there may be scope to expand the guidance in APER to give more detail of specific scenarios, there needs to be sufficient flexibility to cover all future potential scenarios as well as those that have occurred to date. This is not an area that lends itself to codification"*.

protect myself?

- How do I reconcile my statutory duties as a director with my regulatory responsibilities?
- What assurances should I receive before signing an attestation? How should it be framed? What are the repercussions of getting it wrong?

Prudent SIF holders will strive to do all they can to avoid any form of regulatory criticism or sanction. It is hoped that this handbook serves as a helpful practical starting point in achieving that objective.

2

REGULATORY FRAMEWORK OVERVIEW

he regulatory framework applicable to SIFs (in their capacity as such) essentially comprises[3]: (i) the relevant regulations and guidance (broadly, the SPs and CP); as effectively overlaid by (ii) broader stated regulatory expectations – as, for example, contained in relevant Final/Decision Notices, Upper Tribunal judgments, speeches, and various 'informal' regulatory pronouncements; and (iii) the relevant enforcement regime[4].

A. Regulatory requirements

The starting point for any SIF holder (or prospective SIF holder) wishing to understand the nature and extent of their formal regulatory responsibilities is the APER sourcebook within the Regulator's handbook.

In essence, a SIF holder must observe (and continue to observe while remaining a SIF) each of the following seven Statements of Principle for Approved Persons (SPs)[5]:

---

[3]   The 'fitness and propriety' criteria (contained in the FIT sourcebook) fall outside the scope of this handbook. However, it should be noted that an established failure to discharge an individual's regulatory (APER) obligations might, in turn, call into question that person's fitness and propriety; although this will ultimately depend on the specific facts and circumstances of the case.
[4]   Under which a SIF holder would be pursued by the Regulator.
[5]   Contained in APER 2; and issued pursuant to section 64(1) of the Financial Services and Markets Act 2000 (FSMA).

Statement of Principle 1

An approved person must act with integrity in carrying out his accountable functions.

Statement of Principle 2

An approved person must act with due skill, care and diligence in carrying out his accountable functions.

Statement of Principle 3

An approved person must observe proper standards of market conduct in carrying out his accountable functions.

Statement of Principle 4

An approved person must deal with the FCA, the PRA and other regulators in an open and cooperative way and must disclose appropriately any information of which the FCA or the PRA would reasonably expect notice.

Statement of Principle 5

An approved person performing an accountable significant-influence function must take reasonable steps to ensure that the business of the firm for which he is responsible in his accountable function is organised so that it can be controlled effectively.

Statement of Principle 6

An approved person performing an accountable significant-influence function must exercise due skill, care and diligence in managing the business of the firm for which he is responsible in his accountable function.

Statement of Principle 7

An approved person performing an accountable significant-influence function must take reasonable steps to ensure that the business of the firm for which he is responsible in his accountable function complies with the relevant requirements and standards of the regulatory system.

SPs 5, 6 and 7 are SIF-specific; and it is on these provisions that we focus predominantly, as constituting the most likely foundations of any regulatory investigation.

As can be seen, each of the SPs has been formulated at a (deliberately) high level, designed to ensure that they are as all-encompassing (and non-circumventable) as possible[6]. Variously, each SP contains at least one inherently subjective concept – for example: 'integrity', 'proper standards', 'reasonable steps', 'due skill, care and diligence'.

In turn, the Regulator has issued an associated Code of Practice for Approved Persons (CP)[7] for the purpose of helping to determine whether a person's conduct complies with the SPs.

The CP sets out descriptions of conduct which, in the Regulator's opinion, do not comply with an SP. The CP also sets out, in certain cases, factors which, in the Regulator's opinion, are to be taken into account in determining whether or not an approved person's conduct complies with an SP.

Chapter 3 summarises certain of the more instructive provisions of the CP.

B. Broader regulatory expectations

In the current regulatory environment, the rulebook alone will not paint the full picture of the extent of a SIF holder's regulatory responsibilities. Rarely a week passes without some form of public communiqué issued by the Regulator – for example, an enforcement notice, a guide on good and poor practices, a speech or press release. For current purposes, such pronouncements are collectively referred to as 'regulatory expectations'.

----

[6]   Indeed, in its evidence to the House of Commons Banking Standards Committee (in 2013), the FSA acknowledged that: *"Assessing the reasonableness of steps which have been taken necessarily involves issues of judgment, and is not always straightforward. While there may be scope to expand the guidance in APER to give more detail of specific scenarios, there needs to be sufficient flexibility to cover all future potential scenarios as well as those that have occurred to date. This is not an area that lends itself to codification"*.
[7]   As required under section 64(2) FSMA.

The Regulator has confirmed that authorised firms and approved persons are expected to keep abreast of all relevant regulatory pronouncements; and, where appropriate, to go on to consider what lessons might be learned or whether any responsive actions will need to be taken in consequence. A recent quote from the Head of Enforcement is illustrative:

"We expect all firms to consider the lessons from enforcement cases and to consider not just the specific facts but to look at the root cause of the failures and consider whether similar problems could arise in your business."[8]

Accordingly, SIF holders would be well-advised to ensure that they remain up-to-speed on relevant regulatory expectations. While such expectations may be regarded as less formal than 'hard' rules, they are arguably no less important in practice. Indeed, in numerous enforcement notices of late, the defendant has been specifically criticised for not having learned lessons from previous Final Notices concerning other parties. Put simply, ignorance will not constitute a valid defence.

C. Sanctions available to the Regulator

An established failure by a SIF holder to discharge their regulatory responsibilities can result in one or more of the following sanctions:

- imposition of a financial penalty of such amount as deemed appropriate;
- suspension, for an appropriate period, of 'approved person' status;
- variation of approval, through imposition of conditions;
- withdrawal of approval, if no longer deemed 'fit and proper';
- prohibition order, if not deemed 'fit and proper'; and
- public censure

which will, in turn, likely result in attendant reputational/career damage, as well as, potentially, personal bankruptcy.

---

[8]   Tracey McDermott, Head of FCA Enforcement Division, June 2014.

Link to 'fitness and propriety'

It does not automatically follow that an individual found to have breached an SP[9] will consequently fail the 'fitness and propriety' requirement for approved persons. However, any firm employing an individual who is found to have breached an SP, would be well-advised to consider (and be seen to have considered) whether such individual remains 'fit and proper', notwithstanding their breach[10]. In so doing, the firm would be expected to take into account the nature and extent of the breach – for example, whether the breach involved a lack of probity or some 'lesser' form of misconduct. Where a firm concludes that the individual does remain 'fit and proper', a record should be made of the basis of that determination. The firm might also prudently assume that the Regulator will pose the 'fit and proper' question; and should therefore ensure that it can evidence that this issue was actively considered and the basis of the conclusion reached.

D. Enforcement considerations

In practice, any regulatory enforcement action against a SIF holder[11] (in their capacity as such) will be founded upon a suspected breach by that individual of one (or more) of the SPs[12]. However, a SIF holder will only be liable where the Regulator can establish[13] – on the balance of probabilities – that (s)he is **personally culpable**.

It therefore follows that the Regulator *may* take disciplinary action against a SIF holder (for alleged breach of their APER responsibilities[14])

---

[9] Or otherwise found to have been knowingly concerned in a breach of a regulatory requirement by the firm.

[10] For example, in assessing whether an individual satisfies the 'honest, integrity and reputation' element of 'fitness and propriety', the Regulator is required to have regard (among other things) to "whether the person has contravened any of the requirements and standards of the regulatory system", which would include the SPs – FIT 2.1.2.

[11] Other than in the market abuse context.

[12] Or, alternatively (or additionally), where the individual is found to have been knowingly concerned in a breach of a regulatory requirement by a firm – ie, where the individual has been so integrally involved in, or effectively orchestrated, such a breach. See, for example, the case brought against Tidjane Thiam (CEO of Prudential) in 2013. However, it is likely that the significant majority of cases against SIF holders will not be brought under this limb – given that the SIF holder is less likely to have been directly/actively involved in any suspected breach.

[13] The burden of proof resting on the Regulator.

[14] Which, for the avoidance of doubt, excludes the market abuse regime, to which different criteria apply.

only where there is evidence of *personal culpability* underlying the suspected breach. The italicised terms are considered below.

'May'

When deciding whether to take action against a SIF holder, the Regulator will take into account a number of considerations, including (but not limited to)[15]:

(1) The SIF holder's position and responsibilities. The more senior the SIF holder responsible for the misconduct, the more seriously the Regulator is likely to view the misconduct, and therefore the more likely it is to take action against that individual.

(2) Whether disciplinary action against the firm rather than the individual would be a more appropriate regulatory response.

(3) Whether disciplinary action would be a proportionate response to the nature and seriousness of the breach by the SIF holder.

(4) The nature, seriousness and impact of the suspected breach – including:

    (a) whether the breach was deliberate or reckless;

    (b) the duration and frequency of the breach;

    (c) whether there are a number of smaller issues, which individually may not justify disciplinary action, but which do so when taken collectively; and

    (d) the loss or risk of loss caused to consumers or other market users.

(5) The conduct of the individual after the alleged breach – including:

    (a) how quickly, effectively and completely the individual brought the breach to the attention of the Regulator;

    (b) the degree of cooperation the individual showed during the investigation of the breach; and

    (c) any remedial steps the individual has taken in respect of the breach.

---

[15] DEPP 6.2.

(6) The individual's previous disciplinary record and compliance history.

Accordingly, a suspected breach of a SIF holder's responsibilities will not necessarily – but **may** – lead to a regulatory enforcement action against that individual.

'Personal culpability'

Personal culpability arises either where: (i) the individual's behaviour was deliberate; or (ii) where their standard of conduct was **below that which would be reasonable in all the circumstances** at the time of the conduct concerned.

In determining whether or not a SIF holder's conduct was 'reasonable in all the circumstances', the Regulator will take into account (among other things)[16]:

(1) whether the individual exercised **reasonable care** when considering relevant available information;

(2) whether (s)he reached a **reasonable conclusion** on which (s)he acted;

(3) the knowledge the SIF holder **had, or should have had**, of regulatory concerns, if any, arising in the business under their control;

(4) the nature, scale and complexity of the business under management; and

(5) the specific role and responsibility of the individual concerned.

Therefore, disciplinary action will not be taken against a SIF holder simply because a regulatory failure has occurred in an area of business for which (s)he is responsible. The Regulator will consider such action only where the SIF holder's conduct was below the standard which would be reasonable in all the circumstances at the time of the conduct concerned[17]. This is an objective test which – it should be noted – is not necessarily referenced to the defendant's state of mind at the relevant time. In other words, an individual's conduct could be held to have

---

[16]   APER 3.3.1E.
[17]   DEPP 6.2.7G.

been unreasonable in the circumstances, notwithstanding that (s)he may at the relevant time have had the very best of intentions.

In reality, the majority of enforcement cases brought by the Regulator against SIF holders are therefore likely to hinge on the following key issue:

"Whether or not the SIF holder's conduct was reasonable in all the circumstances."

'Reasonabless' is, however, an inherently subjective concept; and is likely to be assessed by the Regulator, applying hindsight judgement. In practice, this assessment will often prove difficult for an individual to challenge; **absent a strong argument that the SIF holder took such measures as could reasonably have been expected in the particular circumstances**. Put another way, a SIF holder accused of unreasonable conduct (and consequent breach of the SPs) **must be in a position to evidence that they did everything they reasonably ought to have done in the circumstances** – if they are to stand a realistic chance of successfully refuting the Regulator's allegations.

On a practical level, therefore, prudent SIF holders will routinely be considering **what further measures they could reasonably be expected to take in the particular circumstances**. Or, put another way, asking "what could I legitimately be criticised for having not done in the circumstances?".

Ideally, this thought process would (where appropriate) be accompanied by a documentary record of the measures taken (including any assurances received) and the basis upon which any ultimate decisions were made or courses of actions pursued.

Chapter 4 elaborates on this theme and offers some practical guidance and 'food for thought' for SIF holders.

Case studies

What do 'reasonable steps' look like?

A CEO (with the CF3 designation) is required to provide a written attestation to the Regulator relating to his firm's compliance with certain conduct of business requirements. The CEO takes it upon himself to review all recent relevant regulatory correspondence and pronouncements – to verify that his firm is indeed operating in line with prevailing expectations. Additionally, the CEO seeks (and duly receives) satisfactory assurances from each of the key relevant internal stakeholders, including the Head of Compliance and business line senior managers.

Notwithstanding the various internal confirmations received and underlying work undertaken, the CEO harbours a residual doubt that he may still not have a sufficient grasp of the 'enterprise-wide' ('holistic') position across the firm. Prior to signing the requested attestation, the CEO considers what more he might prudently do to satisfy himself of the matters referenced therein.

On reflection, the CEO decides to seek some external professional 'comfort' to assuage his residual concern. He details all underlying work undertaken and assurances received to date; and asks the external professional to play 'devil's advocate' and highlight any evident gaps or weaknesses. The external professional raises a number of valid challenges, prompting the CEO to commission some further work and internal assurances. Upon completion of the additional work and provision of these assurances, the CEO is now satisfied that there is nothing further that he could reasonably do to support the attestation. He signs the attestation, which is then furnished to the Regulator.

Assuming that the CEO in this example had been given no reason to doubt the veracity or quality of the underlying work performed and assurances provided, he ought to be well-placed to respond to any subsequent regulatory scrutiny concerning the attestation. Therefore, even if an aspect of the attestation was later found by the Regulator to have been unsubstantiated, the CEO should still be able to credibly argue – if ever challenged – that he could not reasonably have been expected to do more in the circumstances. In short, that he acted reasonably. The Regulator would have to prove otherwise – something it famously failed to do in the *Pottage* case.

John Pottage v The Financial Services Authority, Upper Tribunal, 2012

Much has already been written about *Pottage*; and it is not therefore proposed to undertake here yet another exhaustive analysis. However, certain features of the case merit discussion in the current context.

John Pottage held the CF3 (CEO) and CF8 (apportionment and oversight) functions at UBS Wealth Management (UK) Ltd, which was authorised by the FSA (as was). The FSA held that Mr Pottage had breached APER Principle 7, in that he had failed to take reasonable steps to ensure that the business of the firm complied with the relevant requirements and standards of the regulatory system. In particular, the FSA considered that the measures taken by Mr Pottage (in response to identified warnings and failings) from the date of his appointment as CEO (in September 2006) through to July 2007 were insufficient and, therefore, unreasonable. In essence, the FSA's case was based on the premise that Mr Pottage should have appreciated sooner than he did that there were serious (and subsequently acknowledged by the Tribunal to be) flaws in UBS's systems and controls, and should have acted sooner to review and remediate. Additionally, the FSA argued that Mr Pottage had not gone far enough and had been too accepting of assurances received.

Famously, Mr Pottage appealed and succeeded in overturning the FSA's findings before the Upper Tribunal. In essence, the Tribunal found that Mr Pottage had indeed taken reasonable steps and could not therefore be said to have breached APER Principle 7. In particular, he had undertaken an initial assessment (upon becoming CEO), during which he:

- conducted detailed interviews with management committee members;
- held meetings with senior staff concerned with risk management

and Legal, Risk and Compliance;

- discussed teams and roles with the Head of Risk and Compliance;
- met global heads of Legal, Risk and compliance;
- met group Internal Audit and discussed its plans;
- met the COO to discuss operational issues;
- consulted his predecessor who had not put him 'on notice' of any matters of particular concern requiring his attention; and
- met the business unit head to understand key issues.

Further, Mr Pottage had also proactively addressed problems as they emerged. For instance, he had:

- appointed a new head of Risk;
- reviewed and enhanced client money controls;
- commissioned a peer review of operations and replaced senior staff;
- added Risk to Executive committee agendas;
- engaged a 'Big Four' accountancy firm to carry out an independent review of asset reconciliations;
- instigated a review of adviser training; and
- introduced solutions to address serious transgressions.

In overruling the FSA's initial determination against Mr Pottage, the Tribunal concluded that:

(i) Mr Pottage's initial assessment was reasonable – and that there was insufficient information apparent to him to indicate that he needed to undertake a more comprehensive investigation earlier on (as the FSA had suggested he ought to have done); and

(ii) Mr Pottage investigated every identified control failure; instituted remedies; and took steps to bolster the firm's controls.

In short, Mr Pottage had taken the requisite reasonable steps; and could not reasonably have been expected to go further.

The outcome of *Pottage* can be contrasted with the FSA's case against John Cummings.

John Cummings – where the steps taken were not 'reasonable'

Mr Cummings was the Chief Executive of the Corporate Division of HBOS and held a CF1 (director) function.

After its acquisition of HBOS, Lloyds Banking Group subsequently required a state-backed multi-billion pound bailout in order to remain solvent. The bailout was widely attributed (in part at least) to the financial situation of HBOS' Corporate Division, regarded as the highest risk business area within HBOS.

The FSA alleged that Mr Cummings had instigated numerous transactions with weak lending criteria or aggressive credit structures, at a time when there were serious shortcomings in the Division's control framework. As the individual with specific responsibility for the Corporate Division's strategy and performance, its overall control framework and for managing risks, Mr Cummings ought to have appreciated these failings, and had thereby failed to manage the Division's credit risk appropriately. Moreover, any corrective measures taken by Mr Cummings simply did not go far enough. While the FSA acknowledged that Mr Cummings had not designed the controls and necessarily relied on others, he had nevertheless failed to: exercise proper oversight; heed internal warnings from Group Risk; and ensure that systems and controls were 'fit for purpose'. In the FSA's view, he had also:

- provisioned over-optimistically, despite knowing that impaired transactions were not being appropriately assessed; and
- presided over an environment/culture in which risk management was regarded as an unhelpful business constraint; risk was effectively subordinated to revenue; management oversight was poor; and management information weak.

In short, the FSA concluded that Mr Cummings had not acted reasonably, in that he failed to take adequate measures to bolster the Corporate Division's risk management framework and continued with a high-risk strategy regardless. In other words, Mr Cummings ought reasonably to have done more than he did – in particular, he should have:

(i) ensured that stressed transactions were properly evaluated;

(ii) monitored asset performance and ensured that it was appropriately accounted for;

(iii) mitigated the key risks of weak underwriting and inadequate distribution; and

(iv) set prudent targets and improved credit quality.

Cummings can be differentiated from *Pottage* on two principal grounds:

- while Mr Pottage expressly **acknowledged deficiencies** and **proactively** sought to address them, it appears that Mr Cummings adopted a more passive (and comparatively disinterested) approach; and

- Mr Cummings saw no need to adjust his Division's business model, despite the various 'red flags' concerning its inherent (and unsatisfactorily mitigated) risks. In contrast, Mr Pottage **implemented various business model enhancements** in order to address the perceived weaknesses.

In summary, while Mr Pottage remained 'on the front foot throughout', this could not be said of Mr Cummings, who played an altogether more passive role in events. Ultimately, this appears to have been a key factor behind the differing outcomes. We return to this theme in chapter 4.

E. Directors' dilemma

The heightened regulatory focus on senior individual accountability has prompted a number of regulated firm boards to reassess the duality of their respective legal and regulatory responsibilities.

Legal context

In the UK, a company director owes a set of statutory duties to his company. One of these legal duties is to act in a way that the director considers, in good faith, would be most likely to promote the success of the company for the benefit of its members as a whole. In doing so, a director must have regard (among other matters) to certain additional considerations and stakeholder interests – including, community/environmental impact, employee interests and business relationships with suppliers and customers. It appears to be generally accepted that a director's primary and overriding duty is therefore to act in the interests of shareholders[18]. Further, it is only the shareholders who would be entitled to sue in this context[19].

Regulatory backdrop

As a SIF holder, a director of an authorised firm must additionally discharge certain regulatory responsibilities – which are essentially underpinned by a general concern to ensure that the interests of that firm's clients (or customers)[20] remain appropriately safeguarded at all times. Directors of listed companies – whether authorised or not – will also have specific market-related considerations to factor into their decision-making processes[21].

Moreover, and in furtherance of the FCA's new consumer protection objective, recent regulatory pronouncements[22] make numerous references to the need for firms to put the interests of their clients at the heart of how they run their business; and to ensure that clients' interests are (and remain) central to business models and strategies. Accordingly, from the Regulator's perspective at least, it is abundantly clear that clients' interests are paramount – and not to be subordinated to those of any other stakeholder group (including, shareholders).

With a discernible increase in FCA requests to attend board meetings and/or to review board (or committee) minutes, it is also evident that the Regulator expects to observe – as a reality – the due and demonstrable consideration of customers' interests across boardroom tables.

---

[18] Or, possibly, creditors, for companies in a financial predicament.
[19] Assuming that the company itself opts not to sue.
[20] And, to a degree, market integrity.
[21] Specific consideration of the Listing Rules and Disclosure & Transparency Rules regimes is beyond the scope of this handbook.
[22] For example, the FCA 2013 Risk Outlook and the FCA Business Plan 2013-14.

Relative risk assessment

The results of a recent 'straw poll' suggest that directors of regulated firms believe that the likelihood of a regulatory investigation for failure to discharge their regulatory responsibilities is – in practice – materially greater than that of an action being brought for breach of their statutory duties. Additionally, the directors surveyed considered that the probability of a sanction ultimately being levied (post-investigation) was significantly higher under the regulatory regime. Notably, such sentiments were said to have been influenced by (among other things) the recently-observed increase in regulatory demands for formal attestations from CEOs/boards – a significant and concerning development for many, covered further in chapter 5.

Chapter 4 explores how the apparent divergence between legislative requirements and prevailing regulatory expectations in this context might be addressed in practice.

F. New 'Senior Persons' regime

In response to the perceived regulatory failure to bring certain of the 'authors' of the banking crisis to account, a number of changes have been proposed to the individual accountability regime that applies to banks[23]. The Government has, however, indicated that it will consider (together with the FCA and PRA) whether the new regime should also apply to other financial services firms[24].

In the current context, the most notable aspects of the new regime are:

- a significant increase in the universe of individuals who will have regulatory responsibility and will consequently fall under the Regulator's jurisdiction;

- the reversal of the burden of proof: such that management of banks are presumed to be culpable of regulatory contraventions within their areas of responsibility, unless they can make out a 'reasonable

---

[23] More precisely, deposit-taking institutions and PRA-regulated firms with 'dealing as principal' permission.

[24] Indeed, the FCA has indicated that it would be supportive, in principle, of an extension of the regime to all financial services firms.

steps' defence; and

- a new criminal offence of reckless misconduct in the management of a bank, carrying a maximum sentence of seven years and/or an unlimited fine.

The details of the rules are currently the subject of consultation[25], with a prospective 'go-live' date during 2015 (but as yet unspecified).

The guidance contained in this handbook is equally relevant (to Senior Management Function holders[26]) in the context of the proposed new Senior Persons regime. Indeed, there appears to be little substantive difference in terms of the applicable governing principles and the accompanying indicators of compliant and non-compliant conduct.

---

25   FCA CP14/13; and PRA CP14/14.
26   The broad SIF equivalent roles.

3

CODE OF PRACTICE FOR APPROVED PERSONS

To recap, the CP sets out descriptions of conduct, which, in the Regulator's opinion, do not comply with an SP. The CP also sets out, in certain cases, factors which, in the Regulator's opinion, are to be taken into account in determining whether or not an approved person's conduct complies with an SP.

This chapter considers some of the more illuminating aspects of the CP, with particular focus on the SIF-specific SPs 5, 6 and 7 – as the most likely foundation of any regulatory investigation. We have highlighted in this chapter those items which, based on our experience, can often be inadvertently overlooked; and therefore where SIF holders may be most potentially vulnerable.

At the end of each section, we have posed some practically-focused questions of general application, which SIF holders might usefully address. (Certain of these questions may be more or less relevant, depending on the specific role held.) Alongside, we offer some thoughts and insight. **This chapter is supplemented by, and should be read in conjunction with, chapter 4.**

SP 5

A SIF holder must take reasonable steps to ensure that the business of the firm for which he is responsible (in his SIF role) is organised so that it can be controlled effectively.

The CP identifies examples of conduct that do not comply with SP 5, including (among others):

Apportionment and reporting lines

- Failure to take reasonable steps to apportion responsibilities clearly among delegates; and in respect of all business areas under the SIF holder's control – for instance:
    - implementing confusing or uncertain reporting lines, authorisation levels or job descriptions[27].

Suitability of individuals

- Failure to take reasonable steps to ensure that suitable individuals are responsible for those aspects of the business under the SIF holder's control – for example:
    - failing to review the competence, knowledge, skills and performance of staff to assess their suitability to fulfil their duties, despite evidence that their performance is unacceptable;
        - the SIF holder should satisfy himself, on reasonable grounds, that the nature and extent of any such review is appropriate, the results are accurate and the concerns do not pose an unacceptable risk to compliance with the requirements and standards of the regulatory system;
    - failing to take reasonable steps to satisfy himself, on reasonable grounds, that each area of the business for which he is responsible has in place appropriate policies and procedures for reviewing the competence, knowledge, skills and performance of each member of staff; and

---

[27] Where staff have dual (or multiple) reporting lines, there is a greater need to ensure that the responsibility and accountability of each individual line manager is clearly articulated and understood.

- giving undue weight to financial performance when considering the suitability or continuing suitability of an individual for a particular role.

Temporary vacancies

- Allowing managerial vacancies which put at risk regulatory compliance to remain, without arranging suitable cover (whether internal or external) for the responsibilities; the higher the compliance risk resulting from the vacancy, the greater the steps that are required to fill the vacancy. It may be appropriate to limit or suspend the activity if appropriate cover cannot be arranged[28].

As a general matter, the CP reminds SIF holders that if the strategy of their business is to enter high-risk areas, then the overall degree of control and strength of monitoring reasonably required within the business will be high.

---

[28] Acknowledging that this may have certain commercial or operational repercussions.

KEY QUESTIONS TO ADDRESS	
Question	Comment
• Do I really understand the operational risks inherent in my division/area and emanating from its business model and strategy; and the associated systems of control? • Am I therefore able to assess how my business area is controlled effectively on a day-to-day basis? • Does the management information provided actually facilitate such an assessment? • Are these risks and controls periodically reassessed? • Do I really understand how my business makes its money; and the drivers of its primary sources of revenue? • Is there obvious room for improvement?	A keen understanding of relevant operational risks and associated controls is an effective pre-requisite; and an area of likely focus during any regulatory visit. A failure to display such an understanding may well serve as a 'red flag' for the Regulator. Upon appointment, it will be important for an incoming SIF holder to get a good grasp of the risk and control environment and form an initial assessment as to whether any obvious/significant issues exist. In this context, consideration should also be given to the extent to which reliance can reasonably be placed on any assurances provided by an immediate predecessor. Increasingly, the Regulator will enquire as to the key sources of revenue (by product, division and geography). Management information should not relate exclusively to commercial/financial matters. Periodic reassessments will need to be scheduled and undertaken; as business and regulatory expectations evolve.

Question	Comment
• Do I have a sufficiently strong grasp of the risk management and governance frameworks; in particular, their design, operational effectiveness and any specific weaknesses? • Does the management information provided facilitate such an assessment? • Have these been clearly documented? • Are the risk management and governance frameworks and controls periodically reviewed, to ensure that they remain 'fit for purpose'? • Is there obvious room for improvement?	SIF holders will be expected to be in a position to articulate these frameworks; and to discuss their design and efficacy in practice. Again, a failure to display such an understanding may well serve as a 'red flag' for the Regulator. A simple schematic might usefully be prepared (if one does not already exist), illustrating the risk management and governance frameworks. This might serve as a useful paper to be furnished to the Regulator (if appropriate) during a supervisory visit. It will be important that risk management and governance frameworks are periodically reviewed.
Question	Comment
• Am I comfortable that I would have sufficient visibility over any significant issues or incidents arising within my area of responsibility? • What, if any, formal escalation channels exist? Are these widely known and observed? Do I foster a culture of openness and transparency? • When was the last time that an issue was escalated? • Is there obvious room for improvement?	A SIF holder will be expected to have and maintain visibility over any such issues; and the manner in which they are being handled. This is likely to be facilitated in practice by relevant management information, regular meetings and periodic update reports.

Question	Comment
• Am I satisfied that reporting lines within my area of responsibility are sufficiently clear (and understood)? • How easily could these be evidenced?	A simple schematic, illustrating these reporting lines might usefully be prepared (if one does not already exist). This may serve a number of purposes, including: ensuring clarity; and identifying any gaps, anomalies or issues that need to be addressed. It might also prove to be a useful paper to be furnished to the Regulator (if appropriate) during a supervisory visit.
Question	**Comment**
• Are job descriptions in place for all relevant personnel within my area of responsibility? • Is my own job description up-to-date?	If not, is this really a justifiable position? Consider scheduling periodic (say, annual) reviews to ensure that job descriptions remain accurate and up-to-date; and properly reflect the individual's role and responsibilities. Consider who is best-placed to conduct such reviews*.
Question	**Comment**
• Do I – as a matter of course – assess the on-going suitability of individuals working within my business area; where I have been given reason to believe that their performance levels/conduct are unacceptable? • Would I be comfortable in explaining to the Regulator the nature and extent of the measures that I took? Are these measures verifiable?	Any instances of below-par conduct/performance should ordinarily trigger such an assessment. The Regulator may well wish to understand the firm's response in such a scenario – as this is likely to represent a key cultural indicator for the Regulator.

* Noting that there is no single 'right answer' here.

Question	Comment
• Am I satisfied that appropriate policies and procedures are in place for reviewing the competence, skills, knowledge and performance of each relevant individual within my area of responsibility? • Are these sufficiently clear and demonstrable? • How comfortable would I feel in describing these to the Regulator?	Consider when these were last reviewed; and whether they meet prevailing regulatory expectations. For example, does good (client-focused) compliance conduct feature sufficiently prominently within the appraisal process? Or are all metrics of a solely/predominantly commercial nature – for instance, related principally to revenue generation? This is also likely to represent a key cultural indicator for the Regulator.

Question	Comment
• Am I alive to the risks of allowing managerial posts to remain vacant; without appropriate cover?	This is an obvious area of potential challenge; and it is important to ensure that a credible contingency plan is implemented in a timely manner, where necessary. Any perception of complacency is susceptible to regulatory scrutiny and potential criticism.

A SIF holder must exercise due skill, care and diligence in managing the business of the firm for which he is responsible (in his SIF role).

The CP contains the following (non-exhaustive) examples of conduct that will not comply with SP 6:

Knowledge of the business

- Failure of the SIF holder to take reasonable steps to adequately inform himself about the affairs of the business for which he is responsible – including:
  - permitting transactions or business expansion without a sufficient understanding of the inherent risks;
  - inadequately monitoring highly profitable or unusual transactions or business practices;
  - accepting implausible or unsatisfactory explanations from subordinates or delegates without testing their veracity;
  - failing to obtain independent, expert opinion, where appropriate; for example:
    - if an issue raises questions of law or interpretation, the SIF holder may need to take legal advice. If appropriate legal expertise is not available in-house, it may be appropriate to appoint a suitable external adviser.

Delegation

- Delegating the authority for dealing with an issue or a part of the business to an (internal or external) party/person without reasonable grounds for believing that the delegate had the necessary capacity, competence, knowledge, seniority or skill to deal with the issue or to take the authority for dealing with part of the business;
  - for instance, if the Compliance department only has sufficient resources to deal with 'business-as-usual' issues, it would be unreasonable to delegate to it the resolution of a complex or unusual issue without ensuring that it had sufficient capacity to deal with the matter adequately.

- Failing to take reasonable steps to maintain an appropriate level of understanding about an issue or part of the business that the SIF holder has delegated to another party/person – including:
  - disregarding an issue or part of the business once it has been delegated;
  - failing to require adequate reports once the resolution of an issue or management of part of the business has been delegated.
- Failing to supervise and monitor adequately the person(s) (whether in-house or external) to whom responsibility for dealing with an issue or authority for dealing with part of the business has been delegated – for example:
  - failing to take personal action where progress is unreasonably slow, or where implausible or unsatisfactory explanations are provided; for example, this might include increasing the resource applied, reassigning the resolution internally or obtaining external assistance;
  - failing to review performance of an outside contractor in connection with the delegated issue or business.

Although a SIF holder may delegate the resolution of an issue, or authority for dealing with a part of the business, **he cannot delegate responsibility for it**. It is his responsibility to ensure that he receives progress reports and questions those reports where appropriate, in order to maintain a sufficient degree of oversight.

As a general matter, the larger and more complex the business, the greater the need for clear and effective delegation and reporting lines.

The Regulator recognises that a SIF holder will have to exercise his own judgement in deciding how issues are dealt with; and that in some cases the judgement will, with the benefit of hindsight, be shown to have been wrong. For example, a SIF holder will not be in breach of SP 6 unless he fails to exercise **due and reasonable consideration** before he delegates the resolution of an issue or authority for dealing with a part of the business and fails to reach a **reasonable conclusion**.

Where an issue raises significant concerns, a SIF holder should act **clearly** and **decisively**. If appropriate, this may involve suspending members of staff or relieving them of all or part of their responsibilities.

KEY QUESTIONS TO ADDRESS	
Question	**Comment**
• Is there sufficient focus on risk and clients – for example, when contemplating new business opportunities? • Is the management information provided sufficiently informative in this respect? • How often do I liaise/meet with Compliance and Risk? Is this often enough? • Is there obvious room for improvement? • Do I challenge and ask searching questions, where necessary?	The Regulator may well wish to see demonstrable evidence – for example, through minutes and management information – that risk considerations are featuring prominently during the ordinary course of business. Put another way, the Regulator would likely react adversely to any perception that the interests of a firm's clients were being effectively subordinated to its own commercial interests.
Question	**Comment**
• Am I consciously alert to 'red flags' – for example: unusual transactions or practices; worrying trends; inordinately profitable products; unsatisfactory or implausible explanations from delegates or third party associates? • Do I challenge and ask searching questions, where necessary? For example, around seemingly implausible explanations.	Such 'red flag' issues might usefully be covered in awareness training (to the extent that they are not already).

Question	Comment
• Am I satisfied that appropriate due diligence was undertaken prior to delegating an issue or aspect of the business? • How comfortable would I feel in articulating (and demonstrating) this to the Regulator? • When delegating, is sufficient thought given to the delegate's capacity to perform the delegated task(s)? • How comfortable would I feel in articulating (and demonstrating) this to the Regulator?	A pre-delegation protocol, incorporating a practical checklist, might usefully be considered (if one does not already exist). Such a protocol might cover (among other things): • the delegate's specifically relevant credentials and expertise; and proven track-record; • the delegate's capacity and capability for the role in question; • the form of agreement in place with the delegate – which would ordinarily be expected to include (among other things): provisions affording the delegating firm supervision/monitoring rights; periodic reporting/ MI requirements; appropriate termination rights; service level standards; and resource commitment.
Question	**Comment**
• Do I appreciate the value in obtaining an independent expert opinion, where appropriate – for example, that it may serve as the foundation of any defence to any subsequent regulatory challenge? • Do the potential benefits outweigh any costs? • If ever challenged by the Regulator, would I regret not having sought such expert guidance?	Significantly, in a number of recent enforcement actions, the Regulator has specifically criticised the defendant for failing to seek proper specialist advice. Indeed, it is questionable whether the Regulator would ever have brought these cases had expert advice been sought (and followed).

Question	Comment
• What on-going oversight do I maintain over delegates and delegated issues/business? • Do I challenge and ask searching questions, where necessary? For example, around seemingly implausible explanations or late reports. • How comfortable would I feel in articulating (and demonstrating) this to the Regulator? • Is there obvious room for improvement?	Such oversight might be manifested through, for example: receipt of regular reports and/or management information; periodic catch-up meetings; and scheduled performance review sessions.

Question	Comment
• Do I appreciate that responsibility cannot be delegated?	A relatively common misapprehension under which numerous SIF holders seemingly continue to operate.

Question	Comment
• Where an issue arises, am I confident that I would respond decisively and robustly (and be seen to respond as such)? • Would I be inclined to challenge and ask searching questions – for example, around provisional conclusions reached, assurances provided etc? • How would I evidence this, if challenged?	The response to an issue or incident will often serve as a key cultural indicator for the Regulator. It is therefore essential that any such response is seen to be sufficiently robust and can be readily evidenced.

SP 7

A SIF holder must take reasonable steps to ensure that the business of the firm for which he is responsible in his SIF role complies with the relevant requirements and standards of the regulatory system.

The CP includes the following (non-exhaustive) list of conduct that the Regulator considers would amount to a breach of SP 7.

- Failing to take reasonable steps to implement (either personally or through a Compliance or other department) adequate and appropriate systems of control to enable the SIF holder's business area to comply with the relevant regulatory requirements and standards – these should include:
  - operating procedures and systems which include well-defined steps for complying with the detail of relevant regulatory requirements and standards and for ensuring that the business area for which the SIF holder is responsible is run prudently.

- Failing to take reasonable steps to monitor (either personally or through a Compliance or other department) the SIF holder's business area's compliance with the relevant regulatory requirements and standards.

- Failing to take reasonable steps adequately to inform himself of the reason why significant breaches (whether suspected or actual) of the relevant regulatory requirements and standards may have arisen within his business area – for instance:
  - failing to investigate what systems or procedures may have failed including, where appropriate, failing to obtain an expert opinion on the adequacy of the systems and procedures.

- Failing to take reasonable steps to ensure that procedures and systems of control are reviewed and, if appropriate, improved, following the identification of significant breaches (whether suspected or actual) within his business area of the relevant regulatory requirements and standards – for example:
  - failing to implement in a timely manner reasonable recommendations for improvements in systems and procedures – unless there are good reasons not to;

- what is reasonable will depend on the nature of the inadequacy and the cost of the improvement. It will be reasonable for a SIF holder to carry out a cost benefit analysis when assessing whether the recommendations are reasonable.

It is important to note that the Regulator expects a SIF holder to take reasonable steps to ensure **both**: (i) compliance of his business area with the relevant requirements and standards of the regulatory system; **and** (ii) that all staff are made aware of the need for compliance.

KEY QUESTIONS TO ADDRESS	
Question	**Comment**
• Do I fully appreciate the key regulatory requirements (and expectations) relevant to my area of responsibility? For example, am I familiar with any recently-issued statements of good and poor practice, relevant to my area of responsibility? • Could I comfortably articulate these to the Regulator, if required? • Do I receive periodic (and meaningful) refresher training? When was my last training session? • Do I have knowledge gaps which need to be plugged?	This is a relatively common area of enquiry during supervisory visits. A weak response will likely serve as a catalyst for concern for the Regulator. The demand for periodic refresher training and awareness sessions (in particular, on regulatory 'hot-spots') has increased markedly of late; and is now widely regarded as an essential aspect of working within a regulated environment (as well as being an 'easy-win').
Question	**Comment**
• Do my staff fully appreciate the key regulatory requirements (and expectations) relevant to my area of responsibility? • Could they articulate these to the Regulator, if required?	Increasingly during supervisory visits, the Regulator is making impromptu requests to speak with more junior members of staff. Inconsistent and/or weak responses may leave the firm vulnerable to accusations of poor culture; and weak systems and controls.

Question	Comment
• Do my staff receive periodic (and meaningful) refresher training? When was their last training session? • Is there obvious room for improvement?	Again, periodic training and awareness sessions will play a key role. Training is viewed as a key control and is an effective pre-requisite. A failure to provide adequate training will leave a SIF holder (and his firm) open to regulatory criticism (and potential reputational embarrassment).

Question	Comment
• Do I understand (and could I articulate) what operating procedures and systems have been implemented to ensure that these key regulatory requirements are met? • Do I maintain a 'watching brief' on such procedures and systems; to ensure that they remain 'fit for purpose'? • In practice, what does this entail? For example, what form(s) of assurance do I receive; from whom; and how regularly? • Do I challenge and ask searching questions, where necessary? • Are there any 'legacy' issues, which remain unresolved? • Is there any obvious scope for improvement?	SIF holders are expected to be in a position to articulate and discuss these controls (and how they are monitored); which the Regulator regards as fundamental. Upon appointment, it will be important for a SIF holder to check that any 'legacy' risk or compliance issues have been satisfactorily resolved. More generally, it will also be important for an incoming SIF holder to get a good grasp of the compliance landscape and form an initial assessment as to whether any obvious/significant issues exist. In this context, consideration should also be given to the extent to which reliance can reasonably be placed on the conduct of, or any assurances provided by, an immediate predecessor.

Question	Comment
• Am I satisfied that compliance monitoring activity (including, nature and frequency) is appropriate for my business area? • Could I explain (and justify) this monitoring activity to the Regulator, if asked? For example, do I know what monitoring activity takes place in practice and by whom? • How often is the sufficiency of compliance monitoring activity reviewed; and by whom? Am I satisfied that this is appropriate? • Is there obvious room for improvement?	Again, SIF holders should be well-appraised of, and be able to readily discuss, such monitoring activity. A failure to provide a convincing account may lead the Regulator towards a perception that regulatory/compliance risk is not being taken sufficiently seriously.

Question	Comment
• Would I consciously focus on the underlying cause(s) of a significant compliance breach occurring within my area of responsibility; and then actively oversee any related remedial action? • Could I explain what measures this might involve, in practice? • Would I challenge and ask searching questions, if necessary? For example, around seemingly implausible explanations or late reports.	A SIF holder would be expected to **proactively** probe (and get to the bottom of) the underlying reason(s) of any significant compliance breach. Any 'lessons to be learned' should also be expressly considered. Any necessary remedial actions should be implemented without undue delay; and followed up by a post-implementation review, if appropriate.

In practice, the Regulator may effectively be able to allege breach of more than one SP in respect of the same conduct. For instance, it is not difficult to envisage a scenario in which a failure to exercise due skill and care (as required by SP 6) might also be regarded as a failure to take the requisite reasonable steps to ensure compliance (as required by SP 7). The Regulator's ability to 'pick and choose' in certain circumstances can be illustrated by the fact that Peter Cummings was pursued under SP 6, whereas he might alternatively have been sanctioned under SP 7 (as was John Pottage). Where faced with such a choice, it can be assumed that the Regulator will opt for the particular SP considered to provide the easiest route to a successful determination. In *Cummings*, this was evidently SP 6.

4

PRACTICALITIES – GOING BEYOND THE CODE OF PRACTICE

This chapter builds further upon the provisions of the CP by: (i) offering some generally-applicable practical guidance; and (ii) on a SIF role-specific basis, suggesting various practical steps that might usefully be taken in order to satisfy regulatory requirements and expectations.

Accordingly, this chapter (together with, and supplementing, chapter 3) may serve both as a helpful practical framework for SIF holders; and a convenient benchmark against which they might periodically self-assess.

A. Practical considerations – general

This section is relevant to all SIF holders, regardless of their specific role.

The importance of 'demonstrability'

SIF holders will stand the best chance of refuting any regulatory challenge, if they are able to point to 'hard' (ie, documentary) evidence, underpinning the reasonableness of their conduct (which, as discussed earlier, is likely to represent the basis of any defence). Indeed, recent experience suggests that SIF holders who are unable to corroborate their defence with any such evidence are unlikely to be able to satisfy the Regulator of the reasonableness of their conduct. In other words, the Regulator may well doubt whether an event really happened, if there is no supporting documentary evidence. An unfair working presumption perhaps, but reality nonetheless.

Translated into practice, this will mean the SIF holder being able **to demonstrate** that – for example:

- relevant/material issues were given due (and balanced) consideration;
- advice was sought, where appropriate – whether internally from, say, Legal or Compliance; or externally, from counsel;
- assurances were received, as appropriate, from relevant stakeholders and functions.

Where possible, relevant matters would be evidenced through meeting minutes, file notes and other forms of documentary correspondence/records. While this does not of course mean that every last piece of dialogue, deliberation and thought process must be studiously recorded, it does, nevertheless, require an on-going awareness of those matters or issues most likely to attract subsequent regulatory scrutiny[29]. SIF holders would be well advised to ensure that **these** matters are indeed properly documented.

Adopting the right mind-set

From a risk mitigation perspective, SIF holders would ideally approach their roles with:

- a concerted and discernible focus on clients' best interests; never allowing these to be (or even to be perceived as being) effectively subordinated to the firm's own commercial interests;
- a conscious and consistent regard to the following questions: 'How would this look to the Regulator?', 'How comfortable would I feel if I had to justify this course of conduct?', 'Have I cut any obvious corners?';
- an appreciation that, as time passes and developments occur, periodic 'take stock' reviews will inevitably be required – for example, systems and controls will need to evolve as risks change. While this undoubtedly requires a degree of discipline, it has become an effective pre-requisite for SIF holders. In short, there is no room for complacency;
- an awareness that the Regulator expects you to be focused on (and

---

[29] This handbook is designed to assist SIF holders in this regard.

speak in terms of) risks and attendant controls;

- a desire to ensure that they are kept abreast of, and understand, prevailing regulatory expectations; and, in particular, appreciate 'where the Regulator is coming from' on topical issues of the day (for example, culture and conduct risk); and
- a healthy scepticism – for example, raising challenges and posing searching questions, where appropriate.

While, for many, this may require an adjustment to a mind-set that feels somewhat 'unnatural', prudent SIF holders wishing to manage their own personal regulatory exposure would be well advised to think in these terms.

Handling regulatory interviews

In the current regulatory environment, the likelihood of a SIF holder having, at some point, to attend an interview with the Regulator is high – whether that is as part of the initial approval process; during a supervisory or thematic visit; or, possibly, within the context of an enforcement action.

What to expect

Whatever the context of the interview, it is likely that there will be multiple interviewers, often representing different areas from within the Regulator's organisation – for instance, Authorisations, Supervision or Enforcement.

It would be prudent to assume a challenging session; anything less can be regarded as a bonus.

Preparation

Interviewees should also be prepared for differing levels of industry and firm-specific knowledge to be displayed from within the interviewing team. It may, for instance, be necessary to explain, at a relatively fundamental level, what type of business is undertaken, how and by whom, how the firm/business is structured and how it operates in practice.

Interviewees should ensure that they have read and digested any internal document packs supplied to assist them with their preparations. It would also be helpful for interviewees to be readily able to discuss: the remit of any committees on which they sit; the risk management and governance frameworks; how any pre-existing significant issues are being handled; and any particularly pertinent recent regulatory developments.

Key messages to be conveyed

Ordinarily, it will be important for certain key messages to be conveyed during any regulatory interview – for example:

- I understand my role and can articulate my attendant regulatory responsibilities;
- I take my regulatory responsibilities very seriously;
- I understand (and can describe at a high level, at least) the firm's risk management and governance frameworks;
- I have a strong awareness of the key inherent risks posed by my business; and the related controls employed to manage those risks;
- I appreciate the importance of a strong regulatory compliance culture, driven from the top;
- wherever possible, I can back up my responses with recent practical illustrations – actions speak louder than words!;
- I (and the firm) have a concerted client-centric focus – with clients' interests at the heart of our business model and strategy; I am aware of the key potential conflicts of interest arising within my area of responsibility and can explain how these are managed in practice;

- I have a good grasp of relevant regulatory 'hot-spots' and areas of current concern; and
- I challenge regularly and do not blindly rely.

Dos and don'ts during the interview

Do:

- convey an overall impression of openness and willingness to cooperate;
- provide clear, factual responses to the questions;
- contextualise responses, where appropriate;
- provide practical illustrations to support responses;
- ask for clarification, if unsure; and
- correct any apparent interviewer misapprehensions.

Don't:

- appear defensive or evasive – which may arouse a degree of suspicion;
- feel obliged to fill in awkward pauses/silences;
- go 'off-piste' and digress;
- become argumentative or get drawn into protracted debates; and
- 'bluff' a response, if you do not know the answer – instead refer the interviewer(s) to the person best-placed to answer.

Setting the right 'tone from the top'

SIF holders are expected to lead – and be seen to lead – by example. In practice, this is likely to involve demonstrable conduct through which the SIF holder can be seen to be setting the right 'tone from the top' – for example:

- periodic communiqués to staff, reinforcing the importance of regulatory compliance; and a low tolerance threshold for any contraventions;

- robust treatment of any significant issues (including matters of a disciplinary nature); and
- the imposition of meaningful sanctions in response to any compliance/procedure-related issues (such as non-completion of mandatory training; and repeated PA dealing breaches).

B. Practical considerations – specific SIF roles

This section focuses upon the following SIF roles and offers some role-specific guidance; having regard (among other things) to any lessons to be learned from relevant published enforcement actions: Chief Executive Officer (CF3); Director (CF1), Non-Executive Director (CF2); and Compliance Oversight (CF10).

Chief Executive Officer (CF3)

Much of the guidance in chapter 3, will be of clear direct application to CEOs. This section serves as an effective 'overlay'.

Initial assessments

The importance of an incoming CEO undertaking an initial assessment (of the design and operational effectiveness of the governance and risk management frameworks) was underscored in *Pottage*[30]. Indeed, the initial assessment conducted by Mr Pottage formed the key basis upon which he was found to have taken the necessary 'reasonable steps'.

Of course, the precise nature and extent of any such initial assessment will vary, dependent upon the type, scale and relative complexity of the business. Additionally, a key determinant of the scope and depth of any initial review will be the significance and magnitude of any known compliance or risk issues. Accordingly, a CEO will be expected to have undertaken a proportionately wider and more rigorous review where known material issues exist.

[30] Discussed in chapter 2.

Similarly, when there is an indication – albeit not as yet confirmed – of risk or compliance issues, the CEO will be regarded as being 'on notice'; and will therefore be expected to take prompt steps to understand the true position. Again, the nature and extent of these investigatory measures will depend proportionately on the type of issue concerned.

Other 'take-aways' from recent enforcement cases involving CEOs

While every case will turn on its own unique set of facts and circumstances, it is nevertheless possible to discern certain themes from recent enforcement cases brought against CEOs:

- the need for swift, proactive and credible responses to known issues or warning signs – CEOs must avoid any perception that issues are not being treated sufficiently seriously[31] and with the requisite urgency; as illustrated by the *Pottage*, *Cummings* and *Kumagai*[32] cases; and

- any perception that clients' interests and/or risks are being effectively subordinated to profitability considerations may prove to be decidedly unhelpful; CEOs must not be seen to be pursuing profits at all costs[33].

Culture

Culture is (and is likely to remain) a key area of regulatory focus; forming the subject of numerous recent speeches and pronouncements:

"Culture is like DNA. It shapes judgements, ethics and behaviours displayed at those key moments, big or small, that matter to the performance and reputation of firms and the service that it provides to customers and clients.

In many cases, where things have gone wrong... a cultural issue is at the heart of the problem.

---

[31] With personal attention, if appropriate (and sufficiently serious).
[32] May 2012.
[33] See, for example, *Kamugai* and *Cummings*.

We will draw conclusions about culture from what we observe about a firm...[34]"

In particular, the Regulator will wish to see demonstrable evidence of a strong compliance culture being driven from the very top of the firm (ie, at CEO level) and permeating downwards throughout the organisation. With such a pronounced focus on culture, it would not be at all surprising if, in due course, a CEO was publicly sanctioned for (among other things) failing to instil an appropriate culture within his or her firm.

Culture is, however, an inherently nebulous concept and not easily defined. From a practical perspective, culture might most usefully be approached by reference to some commonly-observed key cultural indicators – for example:

- a firm's response to issues and incidents – often a very revealing indicator of organisational compliance culture;
    - this will include ensuring that any follow-up actions or remedial recommendations are effectively and promptly dealt with;
- how complaints are handled – are they treated with sufficient seriousness?;
- incentive structures – is an appropriate balance being struck between the interests of clients and those of the firm?;
- performance management – are appropriate metrics being utilised to assess individuals' performance?;
- demonstrable board and senior management engagement (or lack thereof) in risk and compliance issues;
- quality of management information – evidencing that the right type of information is reaching the right individuals at an appropriate level of frequency;
- approach to training – how seriously is training taken? What checks and balances are in place to ensure that all relevant individuals have received their training? How rigorously is this policy enforced?;
- response to legal or regulatory developments – is the firm sufficiently responsive to regulatory pronouncements and developments?;
- role and status of the Compliance and Risk functions – how

---

[34] 'The Importance of Culture in Driving the Behaviour of Firms and How the FCA will Assess This' Clive Adamson, Director of Supervision, FCA, April 2013.

prominently do the control functions feature within the governance framework? Do they have a meaningful voice; and can this be evidenced?;

- approach to contraventions of internal requirements – the manner in which any such breaches are treated; and

- approach to product development and on-going product monitoring – is appropriate weight being attached to clients' interests throughout the product development process, distribution and beyond into the post-sale phase?

Attestations

Regulatory attestations are considered in chapter 5. For current purposes, it is simply worth noting that the majority of attestation requests to date have – perhaps unsurprisingly – been addressed to CEOs. Accordingly, CEOs would be well advised to consider carefully the import of chapter 5 – especially, since attestations represent arguably the single greatest avenue of potential regulatory exposure for SIF holders.

Director (CF1)

The heightened regulatory focus on senior individual accountability has prompted a number of regulated firm boards to reassess the duality of their respective legal and regulatory responsibilities. Chapter 2E highlighted the apparent divergence between the legislative requirements applicable to directors of regulated entities and prevailing regulatory expectations. In essence, this divergence arises out of the fact that – broadly speaking – relevant legal requirements are underpinned by shareholders'[35] interests; whereas regulatory expectations serve to the principal benefit of clients.

This section offers some guidance as to how these differing responsibilities might be approached at a practical level.

---

[35] Or, possibly, creditors' interests – if solvency is in question.

Dichotomy of interests

The interests of clients and those of shareholders will not always be aligned – indeed, they may often appear to be polarised.

A simple example serves to illustrate this dichotomy: A regulated firm (Firm X) is concerned that its level of profitability has been dipping over recent years in light of harsh market conditions. Shareholders are losing patience and agitating for action. The firm's only realistic chance of remaining in profit is to implement a drastic cost-reduction programme. As a necessary component of this programme, certain control functions will have to be significantly scaled-back – including compliance, risk and internal audit.

The directors of Firm X are, of course, keen to discharge their legal and regulatory responsibilities. However, in such a scenario, these may be viewed as seemingly irreconcilable – particularly, given the inevitable reduction in capacity and consequent effectiveness of the independent control functions, with their client-focused oversight roles. How should the directors respond?

Striking the right balance

A decision to proceed with the proposed cost-reduction programme, as planned, could clearly be seen as serving shareholders' interests – with increased profitability as the principal driver. Conversely, a wholesale refusal to implement the programme could be regarded as beneficial to the interests of Firm X's clients – on the basis that the programme may have a potentially detrimental impact upon clients, by virtue of materially-reduced control function capacity, effectiveness and oversight.

However, each of these approaches could be viewed as effectively excluding the interests of clients and shareholders, respectively – a potentially difficult stance to justify, if subsequently challenged.

The directors of Firm X may therefore decide that the only viable (and appropriate) course is to execute the programme – but only to the extent that clients' interests will, with a reasonable degree of assurance, remain appropriately safeguarded (the Preferred Solution). Such an approach carries the obvious merit of paying demonstrable regard to both client and shareholder interests.

From the clients' perspective: Under the Preferred Solution, the directors of Firm X might be well-advised to obtain satisfactory assurances from all relevant internal stakeholders that the planned cost-cutting measures will not, in fact, be likely to prejudice the interests of clients. In practice, this may involve requisitioning internal reports, intended to explain, cogently and persuasively, how the interests of clients will remain appropriately protected, in light of the proposed cutbacks. For example, the directors might wish to understand (among other things) how the compliance, risk and internal audit functions will continue to be able to ensure that clients' interests will remain satisfactorily safeguarded, notwithstanding the measures envisaged. Accordingly, the member(s) of senior management responsible for these functions might be tasked with preparing a paper for board consideration and to attend the board meeting at which the paper is tabled – to take questions and respond to challenges.

The concerns/issues raised, actions commissioned, and challenges made, by the directors would be clearly minuted; as would the form(s) of assurance received. Ideally, the documented board considerations should, on their face, leave no obvious questions unanswered or doubts unresolved.

From the shareholders' perspective: The interests of shareholders are also taken into account under the Preferred Solution – albeit, in conjunction with the interests of clients. It will be important here for the directors to be able to demonstrate that the ultimate solution chosen was underpinned by a consideration of shareholders' interests – at least, insofar as can reasonably be expected in the particular circumstances. In the current regulatory climate, it would take a brave board to sanction a course of action that it considers will be likely to adversely impact clients' interests – irrespective of the fact that such a decision may have been driven by an honest and well-meaning desire to discharge legal duties to shareholders.

Faced with such a dilemma, the directors of Firm X will need to strike an appropriate balance between: (i) pushing the cost-reduction programme as far as possible for the benefit of shareholders; and (ii) ensuring, with a reasonable degree of confidence, that clients' interests will remain properly safeguarded. In other words, the planned cost-reduction exercise can proceed to the extent that clients' interests remain duly protected.

Few would dispute that the potential repercussions of a regulatory investigation and any subsequent related sanction would likely result in financial and/or reputational damage to the firm, thereby diminishing shareholder value; thus, on one view, making the Preferred Solution somewhat easier to justify, from a legal duties perspective. **Indeed, such an inter-connection will often in practice prove helpful in enabling boards to reconcile their respective responsibilities and to explain the approach taken.**

Interestingly, the potentially divergent interests of clients and shareholders, and the attendant need for a balance to be struck, have expressly featured in regulatory pronouncements of late. In a 2013 speech, Martin Wheatley, Chief Executive of the FCA, observed that firms must strike a balance between profitability and treating clients fairly, while at the same time acknowledging "...the difficulty for firms of balancing prudential soundness and profitability, with good consumer outcomes".

Practicalities

Directors of regulated firms will almost inevitably, from time to time, encounter such legal/regulatory predicaments. While every case will, of course, need to be considered on its own facts, the following practical pointers might usefully be borne in mind in relevant scenarios.

- Striking the right balance – directors should appreciate and understand that an appropriate balance will often need to be struck in practice – the exclusive consideration of one stakeholder group's interests (be it those of shareholders or clients) may prove difficult to justify.

- Demonstrability is key – the importance of well-reasoned written evidence cannot be over-stated. In practice, it will be vital for directors to be able to point to documentary evidence (eg, board minutes) demonstrating:

- that the board acknowledges its legal and regulatory responsibilities;
- that both clients' and shareholders' interests were in fact taken into account;
- how they were taken into account;
- how the ultimate decision was reached – including, for example:
  - key underlying considerations;
  - any qualifications/restrictions/conditions imposed by the board in sanctioning a particular course of action – for example, to ensure that the interests of clients will remain sufficiently well-protected;
  - this may include a post-implementation review;
  - any forms of assurance received by the board – intended to help evidence the measures taken by the board to satisfy itself that all necessary interests are being appropriately considered and safeguarded; and
  - any challenges made by the board and how these were determined.
- If in doubt, advice should be sought[36] – in the current regulatory environment, the Regulator's interest is high and corresponding tolerance thresholds low.

Conclusion

Directors of regulated firms will occasionally find themselves between the perceived 'rock' of regulatory responsibilities and the 'hard place' of statutory duties. The solution will often involve a delicate balancing of shareholder and client interests.

In the new regulatory era, it might prudently be assumed that the Regulator will take a keen interest in such scenarios. As suggested, a

---

[36]   Indeed, a broad analogy might be drawn with scenarios in which boards of companies in financial difficulty will often seek advice on the question of whether they should be acting in shareholders' or creditors' interests.

cogent documented 'audit trail' will be essential. Indeed, it is difficult to conceive how a board might otherwise, in practice, convince an inquisitive regulator – applying hindsight judgement – that its expectations have been met and the firm's responsibilities discharged; or, likewise, persuade disgruntled shareholders that their interests have been duly served.

For some regulated firms and their boards, this may necessitate a fundamental shift in practice and mind-set; for others a more subtle change of emphasis. The Regulator could not have made its (client-focused) stance clearer – directors of all authorised firms would be well advised to take note.

Non-Executive Director (CF2)

"So what are our expectations of NEDs ... we expect that NEDs will:

1. *Have a good understanding of their firm, its strategy, its customers and the types of product that it sells;*
2. *Play their part in identifying potential risks to customers, not just those to shareholders; and*
3. *Provide robust and insightful challenge to executive management on all aspects of the business, including culture.'*[37]

A non-executive director's (NED's) responsibility (and hence potential liability) will be limited by the role that (s)he undertakes[38]. That said, as illustrated by the above quote, it is important for NEDs to ensure that they are acting in accordance with regulatory expectations – in particular, that they challenge consistently and appreciate that their role (in the Regulator's eyes, at least) is to act as a guardian of client interests, by holding the executive to account.

Accordingly, the guidance under 'Director (CF1)' above is also applicable to NEDs.

While it might be said that NEDs are perhaps less obvious/likely 'targets' for the Regulator (than, say, CEOs), they are by no means

---

[37] FSA speech at NEDs conference, 2011. While this speech was made a few years ago, its import holds true today.
[38] SYSC 4.1.14G.

immune from regulatory interest. For example, in 2013, Angela Burns (a NED) was fined and banned for failing to act with integrity. Among other things, Ms Burns was criticised for failing to disclose conflicts of interest and providing misleading information.

Further, with such a strong regulatory focus on culture and challenge, NEDs would be well advised to ensure that they are actually fulfilling the role expected of them by the Regulator – for example:

- gaining a sufficient understanding of the business to allow them to scrutinise effectively the performance of management and to deliver informed challenge;
- being satisfied that the management information being provided to the Board is adequate and appropriate to support decision-making;
- challenging that management information – particularly, if for example, it is consistently indicating that everything is fine;
- providing robust and insightful challenge to executive management on all aspects of the business, including culture. For example, on strategic business decisions, NEDs would be expected to be challenging senior management to ensure that the potential impact on clients and ensuring their fair treatment are considered from the outset; and
- ensuring that, where necessary, they challenge results in meaningful responsive actions and identification of root causes.

Any perceived failure to do so might just tempt the Regulator into launching a convenient enforcement action, used to send a warning message to the wider NED population in furtherance of its continued 'credible deterrence' strategy.

Compliance Oversight (CF10)

A number of enforcement cases have been brought against CF10s over recent years; several of which have involved questionable integrity and competence[39].

Additionally, the following (non-exhaustive) scenarios have obvious potential to attract adverse regulatory interest:

- failure to inform the Regulator of notifiable events;
- failure to challenge the business or a business decision, when given sufficient reason to believe that there was a material risk of non-compliance[40];
- failure to identify evident issues during monitoring activity;
- failure to action (or to cause to be actioned) any such issues, as appropriate;
- failure to act upon reasonable suspicions;
- failure to raise any material compliance-related concerns with relevant stakeholders;
- failure to act appropriately upon any concerns raised by others;
- failure to ensure that the business is kept appropriately abreast of relevant regulatory developments;
- failure to inform senior management of any concerns about the effectiveness/resourcing of the Compliance function; and
- failure to report material issues to the relevant individual(s)/committee(s) within the governance and risk frameworks.

---

[39] For example: *Mark Bentley-Leek* (2013); *Stephen Danner* (2013); *Arnold Eber* (2014).
[40] For example, *Alexander Ten-Holter* (2012) who failed to satisfy himself that an order to trade was not based on inside information, despite the clear risk that it was.

5

ATTESTATIONS

Backdrop

In an interesting development, the Regulator has recently seen fit to issue a host of attestation requests to firms – a trend that can be expected to increase yet further over time[41]. Through such requests, the Regulator requires a specified individual (**almost inevitably, a SIF holder**, such as a CEO) to confirm certain matters relating to their firm's regulatory compliance in a particular context – and sometimes using prescribed-form wording[42]. Attestation requests may be addressed to all firms in an industry sector; or may, alternatively, be firm-specific – for example, resulting from a recent supervisory visit.

Few would dispute that this approach has been motivated (in part, at least) by the expressed regulatory desire to "hold more members of senior management to account"[43], influenced by the public perception that the Regulator has perhaps not proved sufficiently effective in this regard.

The relatively small number of successful enforcement actions brought to date against members of senior management is widely attributed to evidential difficulties in establishing the requisite personal culpability[44]. For instance, in many cases, a CEO (or other SIF holder) will have been several organisational levels removed from the scene of any regulatory failing – presenting an often insurmountable evidential hurdle for the Regulator.

This chapter explores the regulatory risks faced by SIF holders required to provide such attestations to the Regulator and suggests some practical mitigants.

---

[41] Indeed, the Regulator has effectively confirmed as much on numerous recent occasions.
[42] As was the case in 2012, with letters sent to the CEOs of larger institutional asset managers in relation to Conflicts of Interest compliance.
[43] 'Journey to the FCA', October 2012.
[44] See chapter 2D.

Applicable regulation

The more senior an approved person responsible for the misconduct, the more seriously the Regulator is likely to view the misconduct, and therefore the more likely it is to take action against the approved person[45].

In practice, it is likely that attestors will be SIF holders. As such, they will be subject to the SPs discussed in chapter 2. As we have seen, a general theme underpinning these responsibilities is a requirement to exercise a reasonable standard of conduct. In broad terms, this is likely to translate into a need to (among other things):

- take reasonable steps to ensure that the business for which he is responsible has operating procedures and systems, which include well-defined steps for complying with the detail of the relevant requirements and standards of the regulatory system;
- make appropriate enquiries; adequately inform oneself of certain matters;
- duly consider and challenge information presented;
- take due care before delegating;
- arrive at reasonable conclusions; and
- push back on implausible or unsatisfactory explanations.

However, reasonableness is an inherently subjective concept; and will be assessed by the FCA, applying hindsight judgement. In practice, this assessment will often prove difficult for an individual to challenge, unless perhaps an appeal is made to the Upper Tribunal – an avenue that is, in reality, only likely be pursued by relatively few[46]. Significantly, the Regulator can be seen to have applied a high reasonableness threshold in numerous recent cases[47].

For completeness, an attestor is also potentially vulnerable to the

---

[45] DEPP 6.2.6(1)G.
[46] Certainly, if past statistics are indicative. This is perhaps unsurprising, given the length and cost of regulatory investigations and the general reluctance of defendants to pursue matters beyond the initial investigation.
[47] For example, in a number of recent market abuse cases where the statutory 'reasonable belief' defence was pleaded by the defendant – in each case, the Regulator accepted that the defendant had an honestly-held belief, but simply concluded that the belief was not reasonable.

criminal offence[48] of knowingly or recklessly giving the Regulator information which is materially false or misleading – albeit that this imposes a greater burden of proof on, and a higher threshold test for, the Regulator.

Analysis

An attestation serves to bring a specific matter directly to the attention of the attestor, requiring him to take a positive confirmatory action. An attestation that proves to have been unfounded – for example, as discovered during a subsequent supervisory visit – will likely heighten the risk of an enforcement action being brought against the attestor. For instance, it would be open to the Regulator to contend that – based on the facts discovered post-attestation – the attestor had failed to take reasonable steps to ensure that all necessary underlying work had been undertaken, assurances obtained or challenges made, prior to making the attestation. Accordingly, the attestor might more easily be argued to have been personally culpable.

Put another way, the attestor may be viewed as having assumed a specific personal responsibility to the Regulator, through his provision of the attestation – a failure to discharge which (to the necessary reasonable standards) leaves him significantly more exposed to a 'personally culpable' finding.

Furthermore, an attestation might also effectively preclude the attestor from later running any 'defence' (to any subsequent regulatory challenge) to the effect that he was simply not aware of the matter at issue.

Mitigating the risk – practicalities

In order to mitigate the perceived enforcement risks associated with provision of an attestation, an attestor would be well advised to ensure that:

- any delegated work underlying the attestation is entrusted to

---

[48]   Punishable by fine and under section 398 FSMA 2000 (as amended).

appropriate[49] functions/personnel – eg, Compliance, Risk or certain relevant business line heads;

- all necessary areas touched by the attestation have been covered off satisfactorily;
- assurances are requisitioned from all relevant parts of the business/organisation;
- external advice is sought (and attendant comfort received), where appropriate;
- all assurances/comfort received are carefully considered and subjected to a demonstrable challenge process by the attestor;
- if the attestation is being provided on behalf of the Board, it has been duly pre-approved by the directors; and
- there is a good and clear 'audit trail' of the underlying measures taken by the attestor prior to provision of the attestation – demonstrating that all necessary thought and care was applied.

In this way, an attestor should be well-placed to demonstrate (if ever challenged) that he took all reasonable measures; in other words, that he could not reasonably have been expected to do more in the circumstances.

Conclusion

Attestation requests have emerged as a key feature of the Regulator's 'toolkit'; and, arguably, represent the single greatest form of personal regulatory exposure for attesting SIF holders. Attestors should be under no illusions that their confirmations bring with them a heightened risk of a personal enforcement action – in the event that the attestation is subsequently discovered to have been unfounded.

Accordingly, it will take a brave attestor to 'sign on the dotted line', without first having taken measures along the lines suggested to mitigate this risk down to an acceptable level.

---

[49] In terms of capacity, experience and expertise.

6

CONCLUDING REMARKS

Regulatory expectations of SIF holders have never been higher. And this would appear to be no 'empty threat', given the Regulator's clearly expressed intention to bring more SIF holders to account. The political and public clamour for more CEOs and other senior executives of transgressing institutions [to be brought to account] is ringing loudly in the Regulator's ears – and demonstrable results are essential, if there is going to be any appeasing.

The Regulator will be hoping, in particular, that the forthcoming new 'Senior Persons' regime and its increasing utilisation of attestation requests, will serve to provide the key evidential link to the requisite 'personal culpability' – which it has thus far found very difficult (if not impossible) to establish in several high-profile scenarios.

However, as this handbook has sought to illustrate, SIF holders can do much to help themselves and, crucially, to manage their own personal regulatory exposure. In practice, (and as discussed in chapter 4A), this is likely to involve (to a greater or lesser degree):

- an appreciation of the importance of demonstrability;
- a possible re-adjustment of mind-set – for example, with a disciplined focus on clients' interests, retaining a healthy scepticism, and considering how convincingly a proposed course of action or conduct could be explained away to (or would be perceived by) the Regulator, if challenged;
- thorough preparation for regulatory interviews – ensuring that certain key messages are conveyed, if at all possible; and
- setting (and being seen to set) the right 'tone from the top'.

For CEOs, directors, non-executive directors and those responsible for compliance oversight, the role-specific guidance in chapter 4B should be regarded as an effective overlay.

A prudent SIF holder will continually be considering what further steps (s)he could reasonably be expected to take in the particular circumstances. Or, put another way, "what could I legitimately be criticised for having not done in the circumstances?". On the assumption that such questions return positive confirmatory answers, the SIF holder should be on safe regulatory ground – or, at least, should stand the best chance of defeating any regulatory challenge should one ever materialise.

SIF holders might usefully benchmark themselves against the guidance set out in this handbook (and repeat such exercise periodically). SIF holders who take the approach, and adopt the mind-set, advocated should stand themselves in good stead; and accordingly minimise the prospects of attracting any adverse regulatory attention.